Math Around Us

Counting in the City

Tracey Steffora

Heinemann Library
Chicago, Illinois

© 2011 Heinemann Library
an imprint of Capstone Global Library, LLC
Chicago, Illinois

Edited by Rebecca Rissman, Tracey Steffora, and Catherine Veitch
Designed by Joanna Hinton-Malivoire
Picture research by Elizabeth Alexander
Production by Victoria Fitzgerald
Originated by Capstone Global Library Ltd
Printed and bound in the United States of America,
North Mankato, MN

14 13 12 11 10
10 9 8 7 6 5 4 3 2 1

Library of Congress Cataloging-in-Publication Data

Steffora, Tracey.
  Counting in the city / Tracey Steffora.
      p. cm.—(Math around us)
  Includes bibliographical references and index.
  ISBN 978-1-4329-4921-1 (hc)—ISBN 978-1-4329-4929-7
(pb) 1. Counting—Juvenile literature. I. Title.
  QA113.S834 2011
  513.2'11—dc22   2010030755

Acknowledgments
The author and publisher are grateful to the following for permission to reproduce photographs: Alamy pp. 6 (© Danny Manzanares), 7 (© Tim Jones), 9 (© Marmaduke St. John), 10 (© Mike Spence/Greece), 11 (© Jon Mikel Duralde), 16 (© A. T. Willett), 21 (© Blend Images), 23 glossary – bin (© Jon Mikel Duralde); iStockphoto p. 5 (© Rich Legg); Photolibrary pp. 4 (Lauree Feldman/Ticket), 14 (White Star / Monica Gumm/image-broker.net); Shutterstock pp. 8 (© Johan Pienaar), 12 (© aGinger), 13 (© hans magelssen), 15 (© gary718), 17 (© SVLumagraphica), 18 (© A Davis), 19 (© SOMATUSCAN), 20 (© kkymek), 22 (© Adisa), 23 glosssary – crane (© Johan Pienaar).

Cover photograph of colourful taxis in Thailand reproduced with permission of Shutterstock (© think4photop). Back cover photograph of school buses reproduced with permission of Shutterstock (© hans magelssen).

We would like to thank Nancy Harris, Dee Reid, and Diana Bentley for their assistance in the preparation of this book.

Every effort has been made to contact copyright holders of material reproduced in this book. Any omissions will be rectified in subsequent printings if notice is given to the publisher.

Contents

In the City

Numbers are everywhere in the city.

Numbers help us count.

Here are ten birds.

Here are nine boats.

Here are eight cranes.

Here are seven dogs.

Here are six bells.

Here are five bins.

Here are four windows.

Here are three buses.

Here are two fans.

Here is one river.

There are zero cars on the bridge.

There are many people on the
sidewalk!

Things in Groups

Some things come in groups.

Bicycle wheels come in twos.

Traffic lights come in threes.

Fingers come in fives.

What can you count in the city?

Picture Glossary

 **bin** a container that holds trash or recycling

 **crane** a large machine with a swinging arm that picks up heavy objects

Index

Notes to Parents and Teachers
Before reading
The ability for children to recognize numbers is not the same thing as them being able to understand the concept of number, or the quantity that each numeral represents. Gather 45 of the same object, such as pennies. Count from one to nine with a child, pausing at each number to place that quantity of the object in their hand and then having them remove the objects and line them in rows on a table. This will help give children a visual and tactile sense of each numeral.

After reading
Supply a selection of books or magazines that contain urban scenes and have children hunt for objects to count. You can then have children contribute their findings to a large class chart or create counting books of their own. This activity can also be adapted to your own neighborhood or community.